W9-ATJ-363

Swim Fins, 1717
Public Library in America, 1731
Sanitation Department, circa 1736
Lightning Rod, 1752
Home Delivery Postal Service, 1753
Odometer, 1753
Political Cartoon in America, 1754
JOIN OR DIE
Treaty of Alliance (with France), 1778
Treaty of Peace (with England), 1783
Bifocals, 1784
Daylight Saving Time, 1784

Fire Company, 1736
Pennsylvania Fireplace, 1741
Pennsylvania Hospital Co-Founder, 1751
Kite Experiment, 1752
Library Chair, 1761
Writing Chair, 1761
Glass Armonica, circa 1762
Declaration of Independence, 1776
Charted the Gulf Stream, 1768–1785
Long Arm, 1786
U.S. Constitution, 1787

For my son, Benjamin, who reminds me to fill each day with wonder and discovery—Dr. Franklin would be proud of you —Love, Daddy

Special thanks to Neil Di Sabato, Roy Goodman, Neil Ronk, Adam Potkay, Bill Ochester, and Ralph Archbold

SQUARE FISH

Imprints of Macmillan Publishing Group, LLC
120 Broadway, New York, NY 10271

mackids.com

NOW & BEN. Copyright © 2006 by Gene Barretta.
All rights reserved. Printed in China by RR Donnelley Asia Printing Solutions Ltd., Dongguan City, Guangdong Province.

Henry Holt® is a registered trademark of Macmillan Publishing Group, LLC.
Square Fish and the Square Fish logo are trademarks of Macmillan and
are used by Henry Holt and Company under license from Macmillan.

Library of Congress Cataloging-in-Publication Data
Barretta, Gene
Now & Ben : the modern inventions of Benjamin Franklin / by Gene Barretta.
p. cm.
1. Franklin, Benjamin, 1706-1790. 2. Inventions—United States—History—Juvenile literature.
3. Inventors—United States—Juvenile literature. I. Title: Now and Ben. II. Title: Modern inventions of Benjamin Franklin.
III. Title. T48.B27 2006 609'.2—dc22 2005012491

Originally published in the United States by Henry Holt and Company
First Square Fish Edition: 2008
Square Fish logo designed by Filomena Tuosto

ISBN 978-0-8050-7917-3 (Henry Holt hardcover)
16 15 14 13 12 11 10 9 8

ISBN 978-0-312-53569-8 (Square Fish paperback)
30 29 28 27 26 25 24 23 22 21 20 19 18

ISBN 978-1-250-76766-0 (Kiwi Crate paperback)
10 9 8 7 6 5 4 3 2

AR: 5.1 / F&P: O / LEXILE: 910L

Now & Ben

The Modern Inventions of Benjamin Franklin

GENE BARRETTA

SQUARE FISH

HENRY HOLT AND COMPANY
NEW YORK

SON
FRANCIS
SON
WILLIAM
DAUGHTER
SALLY
WIFE
DEBORAH

Now and then, we think about Ben.
Dr. Benjamin Franklin, to be precise.
And we think about his many inventions—
inventions he originated more than two hundred years ago.

It was as if Ben could see into the future.
Almost everything he created is still around today.
For instance . . .

POST OFFICE
BULLETINS
FLIPPERS FOR SALE
CRUISE GULF STREAM
FOOD
HARMONICA
COMICS
POOR RICH
ICE CREAM
SPRING FIELD

Now... our newspapers are filled with illustrations.

Ben... was the first to print a political cartoon in America. The cartoon encouraged the American colonies to join together or die like the disconnected snake.

Now... bifocals are very common. Bifocals combine two sets of lenses into one pair of glasses. The bottom lens helps see near, and the top lens helps see far.

Ben... originally designed bifocals for himself after he grew tired of switching between two pairs of glasses.

Now . . . our world relies on electricity. In the eighteenth century, many people still believed that lightning was an act of anger and punishment from God.

Ben... was one of the scientists who discovered the true nature of electricity and how to use it. He learned that lightning is electricity when he attached a small metal wire to the top of a kite and gathered electricity from a storm cloud.

Now... many buildings and homes use lightning rods to protect against lightning strikes.

Ben... invented the lightning rod and was the first to use it. The pointed iron rod acts like a magnet and grabs an approaching lightning bolt from the sky before it can strike the rooftop. The electricity then travels safely down a long wire into the ground. It prevents fires and keeps dangerous amounts of electricity away from the house.

Now... this gadget goes by many names, such as the Grabber. Everyone has seen one—it's the long stick that helps grab items from out-of-reach places.

Ben... invented the original device and called it the Long Arm because it worked like a very long arm.

Now . . . swimmers and divers use flippers to move faster through the water.

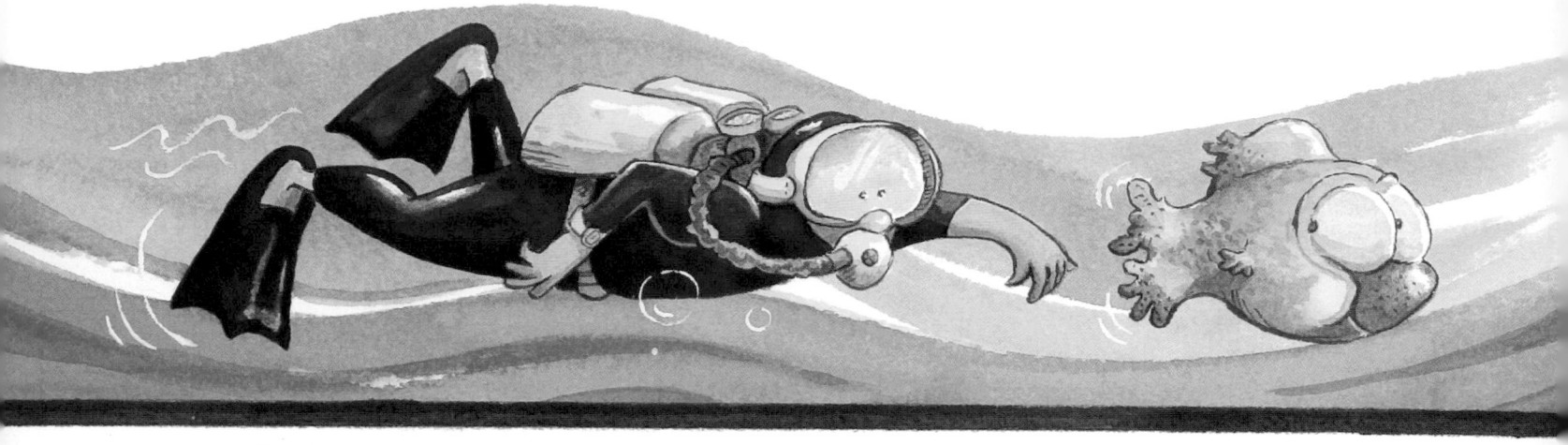

Now . . . ships travel across the Gulf Stream to take advantage of the faster current.

Now . . . we understand and accept the benefits of vitamin C.

Ben... invented things even when he was a boy. He was an avid swimmer and built wooden flippers for both his hands and feet.

Ben... measured, charted, and publicized the Gulf Stream during his eight voyages across the Atlantic Ocean.

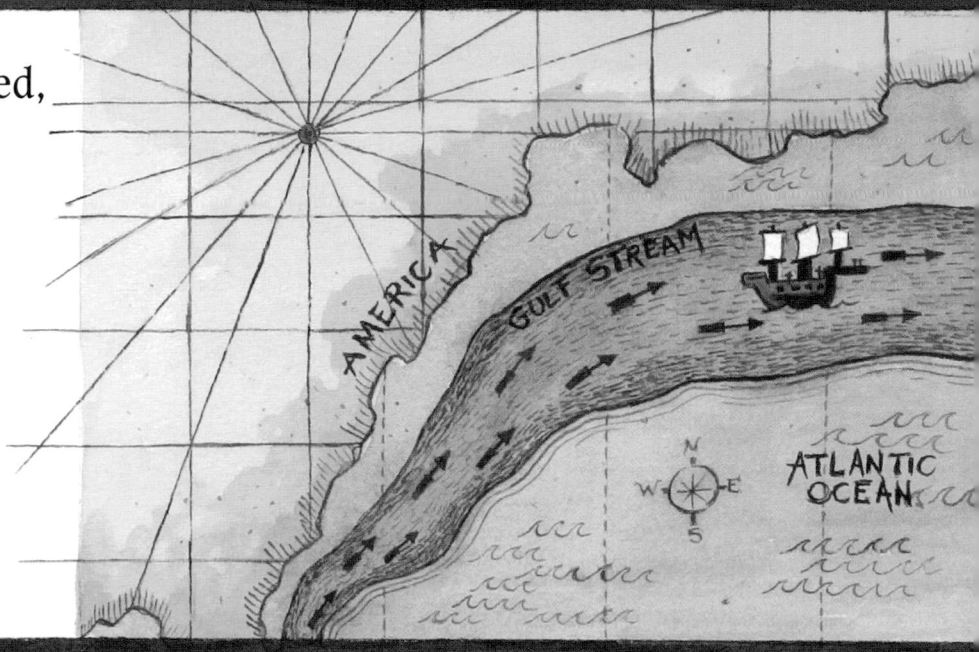

Ben... was an early promoter of eating citrus fruits to help prevent a disease called scurvy.

Now...
for a musical interlude.

Ben... invented the glass armonica. He was able to create music by simply touching his wet fingers to a row of spinning glass bowls. Mozart and Beethoven were so moved by the sounds that they composed for the instrument.

Today, glass armonicas are very rare. You are more likely to find one in a muscum than in a music store.

Now... our fireplaces are very efficient and easy to use.

Ben... improved on the primitive fireplaces of his day when he designed the Pennsylvania Fireplace, later renamed the Franklin stove. He built it with iron to contain the heat from a fire long after the logs were burned. It also sat away from the wall to heat the room more evenly.

The smoke ventilation was not perfect, but later inventors improved it. Before Ben's fireplace, indoor smoke could be suffocating.

Now... chairs come in all shapes and sizes.

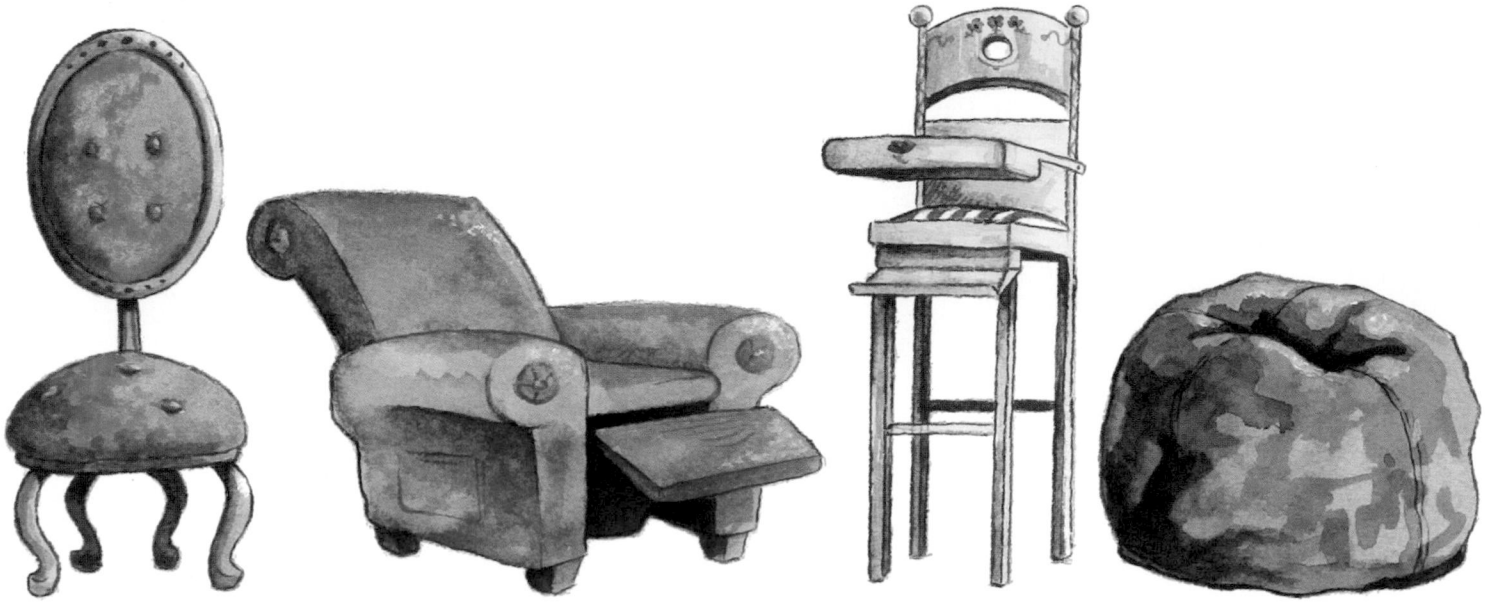

Now... everyone has seen a rocking chair, but not many have seen Dr. Franklin's rocking chairs.

Ben... designed two chairs that are still very useful.

The writing chair combined a desk and chair into one.

The library chair was a combination chair and stepladder.

Ben... invented one rocking chair with a fan on top and one that churned butter.

Now... every year, we observe daylight saving time, which means we set our clocks ahead one hour in the springtime. As a result, it stays darker longer in the morning when most people are sleeping and stays light longer at the end of the day so we can save more energy. In the fall, we return the clocks to standard time.

Ben . . . suggested this idea in one of his essays as a way to save money by burning fewer candles. Farmers could also gain more work time in the evening. Daylight saving time was not officially practiced until World War I, more than a hundred years later.

As for clocks . . .
Ben designed the first clock with a second hand.

Now... every automobile has an odometer to measure the distance it travels.

Ben... invented the odometer when he was postmaster general so he could measure his postal routes.

Now... almost every large community includes a library, a hospital, a post office, a fire department, and a sanitation department.

Ben... lived in a city that had none of these establishments, so he helped organize the first of each.

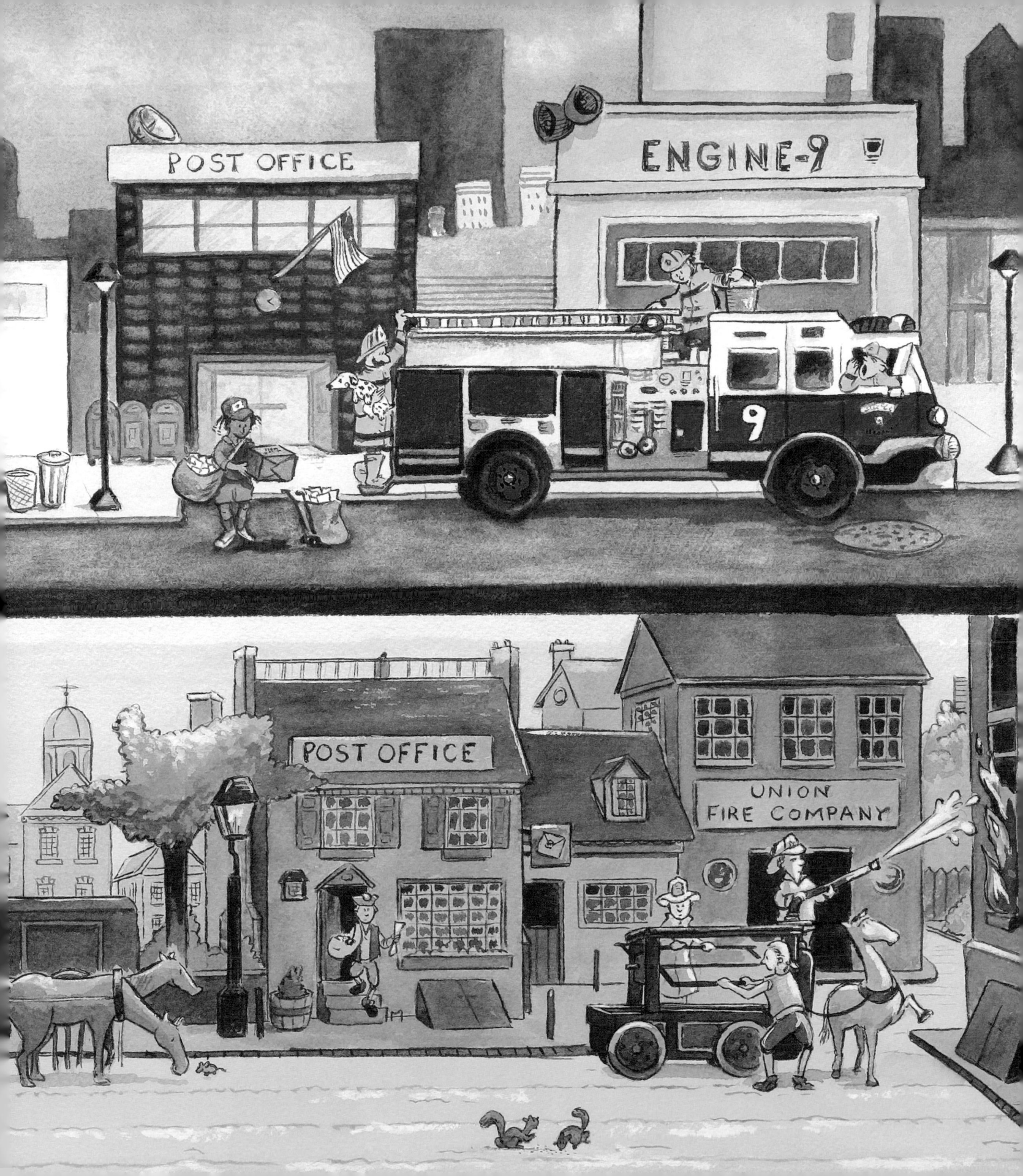
POST OFFICE
ENGINE-9
9
POST OFFICE
UNION
FIRE COMPANY

Now . . . and then, we owe thanks to Ben for his important inventions. But many would agree that his greatest accomplishments came in the form of documents—documents that helped shape the world.

Ben . . . had a pivotal role in developing America's Constitution, the Treaty of Alliance with France, the Treaty of Peace with England, and the Declaration of Independence.

It's remarkable that one man could achieve so much in a lifetime. He has certainly helped to form the modern world. . . .

Will his contributions help to form the future?

GLOBAL NEWS
POST SECTOR
TUBE-O'-TREATS
MUSIC TO GO
SALE
ALEA IS MY GIRLFRIE

Swim Fins, 1717
Public Library in America, 1731
Sanitation Department, circa 1736
Lightning Rod, 1752
Home Delivery Postal Service, 1753
Odometer, 1753
Political Cartoon in America, 1754
JOIN OR DIE
Treaty of Alliance (with France), 1778
Treaty of Peace (with England), 1783
Bifocals, 1784
Daylight Saving Time, 1784

Fire Company, 1736
Pennsylvania Fireplace, 1741
Pennsylvania Hospital Co-Founder, 1751
Kite Experiment, 1752
Library Chair, 1761
Writing Chair, 1761
Glass Armonica, circa 1762
Declaration of Independence, 1776
Charted the Gulf Stream, 1768-1785
Long Arm, 1786
U.S. Constitution, 1787